What Would YOU Do?

Should Wendy Walk the Dog?

Taking Care of Your Pets

Rebecca Rissman

Heinemann
LIBRARY

Chicago, Illinois

© 2013 Heinemann Library
an imprint of Capstone Global Library, LLC
Chicago, Illinois

To contact Capstone Global Library please phone 800-747-4992, or visit
our website www.capstonepub.com

Edited by Daniel Nunn, Rebecca Rissman, and Siân Smith
Designed by Steve Mead
Picture research by Mica Brancic
Production by Alison Parsons
Originated by Capstone Global Library Ltd
Printed and bound in China by Leo Paper Products Ltd

16 15 14 13 12
10 9 8 7 6 5 4 3 2 1

Library of Congress Cataloging-in-Publication Data
Rissman, Rebecca.
Should Wendy walk the dog? : taking care of your pets / Rebecca Rissman.
p. cm.—(What would you do?)
 Includes bibliographical references and index.
 ISBN 978-1-4329-7237-0 (hb)—ISBN 978-1-4329-7243-1 (pb) 1. Pets—
Juvenile literature. I. Title.
 SF416.2.R58 2013
 636.088'7—dc23   2012017431

Acknowledgments
All photographs © Capstone Publishers (Karon Dubke).

Every effort has been made to contact copyright holders of any material
reproduced in this book. Any omissions will be rectified in subsequent
printings if notice is given to the publisher.

Contents

Making Choices 4

Should Wendy Walk Her Dog? 7

Should Henry Clean the Cage? . . .11

Should Bella Feed Her Birds? 15

Should Theo Brush His Cat? 19

Picture Glossary. 23

Index 24

Making Choices

We make choices every day, such as "Should I wear my coat?"

Our choices have effects.

Ask yourself if your choices will have good or bad effects.

Should Wendy Walk Her Dog?

Wendy's dog has been inside all day.

Should Wendy walk her dog?

Wendy could choose to walk
her dog.

Wendy could choose not to walk
her dog.

What Would YOU Have Done?

If Wendy had taken her dog for a walk, the dog would have been able to go to the bathroom outside and get some exercise. If she had not taken her dog for a walk, it might have made a mess indoors.

Should Henry Clean the Cage?

Henry's hamster cage has not been cleaned for two weeks. Should Henry clean the cage?

Henry could choose to clean his
hamster's cage.

Henry could choose not to clean his
hamster's cage.

What Would YOU Have Done?

If Henry had cleaned his hamster's cage, it would have helped his hamster stay healthy and happy. If Henry had not cleaned his hamster's cage, it would begin to smell and his hamster could have become sick.

Should Bella Feed Her Birds?

Bella's birds have not been fed for the day. Should Bella feed her birds?

Bella could choose to feed her birds.

Bella could choose not to feed
her birds.

What Would YOU Have Done?

If Bella had fed her birds, they would have stayed healthy and happy. If Bella did not feed her birds for a long time, they would have become unhappy and sick, and then died.

Should Theo Brush His Cat?

Theo's cat has long fur that has not been brushed for two days. Should Theo brush his cat's fur?

Theo could choose to brush his cat's fur.

Theo could choose not to brush his cat's fur.

What Would YOU Have Done?

If Theo had brushed his cat, its fur would have stayed clean and healthy. If Theo had not brushed his cat, its fur might have become knotted and tangled.

Picture Glossary

choice a decision

effects the results of a decision or something you choose to do. Choices can have good or bad effects.

healthy fit and well

Index

birds 15–18

brushing 19–22

cat 19–22

clean 11–14, 22

dog 7–10

feeding 15–18

hamster 11–14

healthy 14, 18, 22

Notes for Parents and Teachers
Before reading

Explain to children that a consequence is the outcome, or result, of a decision. Explain that different decisions can have different consequences, and that some are better than others. Ask children to brainstorm some decisions they make regarding their pets. For example, *Should I feed my fish?* Explain that the consequences of their decisions are important, and can impact the health of their pet. For example, *Fish need food to stay alive.*

After reading

Turn to page 11. Ask children to make two drawings: one of a clean hamster cage, and one of a dirty hamster cage. Ask children which cage would be best for the hamster and why.